SENSATIONAL SENSES

AMAZING WAYS ANIMALS PERCEIVE THE WORLD

REBECCA E. HIRSCH

Ⓜ Millbrook Press / Minneapolis

To all who are curious about the worlds that lie beyond our senses

Millbrook Press™
An imprint of Lerner Publishing Group, Inc.
241 First Avenue North
Minneapolis, MN 55401 USA

For reading levels and more information, look up this title at www.lernerbooks.com.

Illustrations on pages 13, 20, 21, 24, 27, and 31 by Laura K. Westlund.

Designed by Viet Chu.
Main body text set in Aroma LT Pro.
Typeface provided by Linotype AG.

Library of Congress Cataloging-in-Publication Data

Names: Hirsch, Rebecca E., author.
Title: Sensational senses : amazing ways animals perceive the world / Rebecca E. Hirsch.
Description: Minneapolis, MN : Millbrook Press, [2022] | Includes bibliographical references and index. | Audience: Ages 8–14 | Audience: Grades 4–6 | Summary: "Humans have five senses. But some animals have a sixth sense. From science writer Rebecca E. Hirsch comes a book about extrasensory animals. Discover how animals use their senses to find food, navigate, and communicate" —Provided by publisher.
Identifiers: LCCN 2021011559 (print) | LCCN 2021011560 (ebook) | ISBN 9781728419220 (library binding) | ISBN 9781728445380 (ebook)
Subjects: LCSH: Senses and sensation—Juvenile literature. | Perception in animals—Juvenile literature. | Animal behavior—Juvenile literature.
Classification: LCC QP434 .H57 2022 (print) | LCC QP434 (ebook) | DDC 573.8/7—dc23

LC record available at https://lccn.loc.gov/2021011559
LC ebook record available at https://lccn.loc.gov/2021011560

Manufactured in the United States of America
1-49037-49254-10/26/2021

INTRODUCTION
The World beyond Your Senses

Imagine you're a superhero on a top-secret mission. Disguised in civilian clothes, you pursue a villain as she weaves down a crowded sidewalk. She carries a roll of paper tucked under her arm—the stolen blueprints. You must recover them. You are sure you can catch her, but then she gives you a backward glance, smiles, and disappears into an alley.

When you reach the alley, it is dark and deserted. A dead end. Heavy metal doors line one brick wall. Which one did she go through? You must find out quickly before she gets away. Your ears tingle. You tip your head, tune one ear to the first door, and listen with your super hearing. No one is inside. At the second door, all is quiet. At the third door, you can just hear distant footsteps. That's the one! You yank it open and tear after her in hot pursuit.

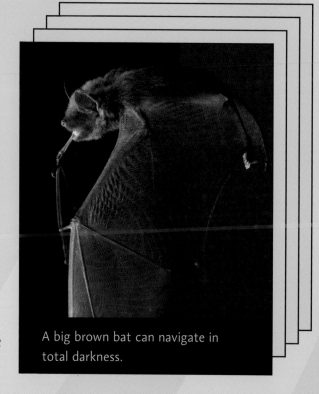

A big brown bat can navigate in total darkness.

In comic books and movies, superheroes use their super senses to track down criminals. But real super senses exist in the world of nature. Some animals have extraordinary ways of perceiving the world. They can see, hear, smell, taste, or feel things that are hidden to humans. Some have sixth senses, special ones that you don't have. Animals use these sensational abilities to evade predators, catch prey, or send secret signals. In nature, super senses aren't just cool to have—they're a matter of survival.

A mantis shrimp, a colorful cousin of crabs and lobsters, rests on the bottom of a coral reef.

Want to wander through the surprising world of supreme animal senses? You'll need your own sharp senses and your keen mind. The animals are ready, waiting for you with their unique ways of perceiving the world.

CHAPTER 1
Star of the Swamp

STAR-NOSED MOLE
SCIENTIFIC NAME: *Condylura cristata*
SECRET HIDEOUT: wetlands of southeastern Canada through the eastern United States, as far south as Georgia
SIZE: up to 8 inches (20 cm) long from star to tail
WEIGHT: up to 2.7 ounces (77 g)
SUPER SENSE: ultrasensitive touch

A dark creature scampers through a tunnel under a swamp. *Pit-pat-pit-pat*. Its body is cloaked in sleek black fur. Its face appears to be under attack by a pack of tiny, wriggling pink worms. Except those aren't worms—that's its superpowered nose. Say hello to the star-nosed mole.

As the creature darts through the dark tunnel, it rapidly pats its supersensory snout along the moist, marshy soil. The nose encounters a soft, pink slug. *Slurrp!* The slug disappears into the mole's mouth. The mole creeps forward, bopping its nose along the ground. *Splat!* The nose touches a grub. *Chomp!* In a blink, the tasty morsel is gone.

The mole will continue all day, finding meals with its sensitive nose. By the end of the day, it will have eaten its body weight in food.

SPEED-EATING CHAMPION

The star-nosed mole lives in marshy wetlands. This swamp dweller digs deep tunnels underground with its sharp front claws, and sometimes it comes to the surface for a swim.

The mole is practically blind, but sight isn't much use in its dark, subterranean world. Instead, the critter surveys the world through its star-shaped nose, a supersensitive organ for touch.

The mole's nose is about the size of the tip of your pinkie. It is made of twenty-two fleshy pink arms, or rays. As the mole blindly scurries through a tunnel, it rapidly presses its nose along the moist soil. With each pat, nerves in the star send signals to the mole's brain.

Duncan Leitch was a student at Vanderbilt University when he wanted to learn more about how that extraordinary nose communicates with the mole's brain. He counted the star's nerve fibers, the individual threads that send signals along the nerves. He added up over 168,000 nerve fibers. By comparison, the palm of your

Star-nosed moles are skilled hunters that find food with their fleshy snouts.

The mole's star-shaped nose is the size of the tip of your pinkie finger.

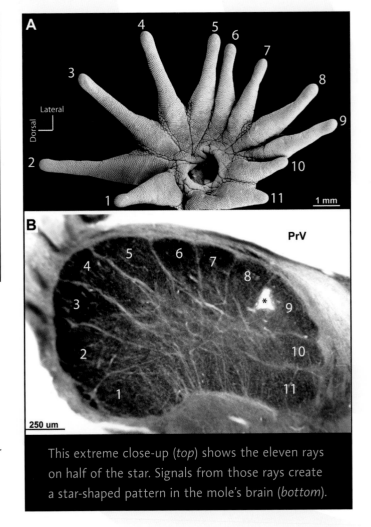

This extreme close-up (*top*) shows the eleven rays on half of the star. Signals from those rays create a star-shaped pattern in the mole's brain (*bottom*).

hand has about 17,000. So the mole has the sensitivity of almost ten human hands crammed into an area the size of your pinkie tip!

Leitch said those nerve signals create star-shaped patterns in different parts of the mole's brain. So each time the mole taps its super snout on the ground, it is creating a star-shaped picture of its surroundings in its brain.

The mole's nose is not only supersensitive, it's superspeedy. With the rays of its fleshy star, the mole can touch up to twelve different objects in one second. High-speed cameras have helped scientists slow this down so they can see and understand how the mole uses its star.

As the mole presses its nose along the ground, the outer rays feel for food. If those rays encounter an object that might be a meal, the mole touches the item with its inner rays. These inner rays are smaller but even more sensitive. This is like how your fingertips are more sensitive than the palms of your hands. If the mole decides the object is edible— snack time!

The mole is a speed-eating machine, moving like lightning to identify and eat everything from insects to mollusks, worms, and small fish. In a little more than a tenth of a second, the creature can touch prey with its snout, decide the prey is edible, pick up the prey with its tweezerlike front teeth, chew, and swallow. That's how long it takes you to blink!

"It happens incredibly fast," said Leitch. "It's one of the fastest [food-handling times] of any animal that's ever been recorded."

Leitch believes star-nosed moles have a lot to teach us about what it's like to experience the world through touch. "They provide a window to understanding that sense in a way that we can't tell in . . . studying ourselves."

He continues to be amazed by sensory superstars like the star-nosed mole. "It's surprising to me getting to look at the diversity of animals and how they can survive in different environments." he said. "There's kind of a unique beauty in all of these diverse creatures."

Underwater, the star-nosed mole is a speedy sniffer.

SLIMY SNOT BUBBLES

The star-nosed mole has another trick up its supersensory snout. It can smell underwater, something no other mammal is known to do. When swimming, the mole blows a small bubble out of its nose and inhales the bubble again. This allows the mole to smell whatever the bubble has touched—like a small fish. *Yum!* As with everything the mole does, its underwater smelling is superspeedy. A mole can blow a bubble and inhale it again in the same time it takes you to take a sniff of air.

CHAPTER 2

Powerful Peepers

MANTIS SHRIMP
SCIENTIFIC NAME: *Stomatopoda*
SECRET HIDEOUT: coral reefs, seagrass beds, sand and rubble flats in temperate, subtropical, and tropical oceans
SIZE: up to 12 inches (30 cm) long
WEIGHT: up to 3.2 ounces (90 g)
SUPER SENSES: color vision, depth perception, and polarized light perception

Two eyeballs swivel on stalks atop the head of a mantis shrimp. *Zip! Zoop!* The eyes move up, down, left, and right as the critter scuttles across the coral reef. He is keeping watch for enemies and looking for a place to hide.

He spies a cranny in the coral. That looks like a promising spot. *Patapatapat.* The bug-eyed creature scoots in for a closer look.

Flash!

Uh-oh! He spies a secret signal coming from the hole. No one else in the coral reef can see the sign, yet the mantis shrimp knows it is a warning. It tells him this nook is occupied by another mantis shrimp—and this one is broadcasting that he is not in a welcoming mood.

Our mantis shrimp is a fighter. He will fight most anything that gets in his way. But so will another mantis shrimp, and one defending its burrow will fight to the death.

Bye! Our mantis shrimp turns and hurries away. He will have to find another place to stay.

EYE SPY

Mantis shrimps, or stomatopods (stoh-MA-tah-pawds), are relatives of crabs, lobsters, and shrimp. These tiny superheroes have the most advanced eyeballs on the planet.

What makes a mantis shrimp's eyes so spectacular? Let's start with how they move. The eyes are mounted on movable stalks, and each eye can swivel in a different direction. So a mantis shrimp can scan a huge area of its environment at once.

Then there's how the eyes take in light. Your eyes each have one area—the pupil—where light enters. Each eye forms a slightly different image. That gives you depth perception, the ability to distinguish distances. But each mantis shrimp eye has three places where light enters.

A mantis shrimp's eyes are divided into three parts: a top, a bottom, and a band in the middle. Each part forms a separate image.

Mantis shrimp have amazingly complex eyes. They can see types of light we can't see, such as circularly polarized light.

Each of these super eyeballs forms three different images, giving a mantis shrimp the ability to judge depth with just one eye. So, if these feisty creatures lose an eye in a fight, they can still see just fine.

Their super vision doesn't stop there. Most people have three color receptors for recognizing red, green, and blue. A mantis shrimp has up to *sixteen* color receptors. This helps them see ultraviolet light, a wavelength of light you can't see. But having so many color receptors doesn't mean these creatures can recognize many more colors than you can. They recognize colors in a different way than you do. Your eyes send color signals to your brain for processing, Then you see not just red, green, and blue but a kaleidoscope of colors. But a stomatopod processes color right in its eyes, not in its brain. So these critters are poor at telling similar colors apart but superspeedy at reacting to what they see.

And speed is an important superpower when you're a mantis shrimp. They have powerful front claws. Their punch is as fast as a speeding bullet and strong enough to break glass. *Crack!* Armed with these devastating weapons, they'll take on predator, prey, or fellow stomatopod.

"Mantis shrimps are extremely violent," says Yakir Gagnon, a scientist at Lund University in Sweden. "They attack everything and anything with great success."

He has studied another amazing aspect of a mantis shrimp's eyes: their ability to see a type of light that's invisible to all other living things. It's circularly polarized light, and it's created when light reflects off a surface in corkscrew-shaped waves. Think of tying a jump rope to a doorknob and holding the other end in your hand. You can send the rope in a spiral by moving your arm around in a circle. That's how circularly polarized light moves. To you, it looks like normal sunlight. But with its powerful peepers, a mantis shrimp sees it as something special.

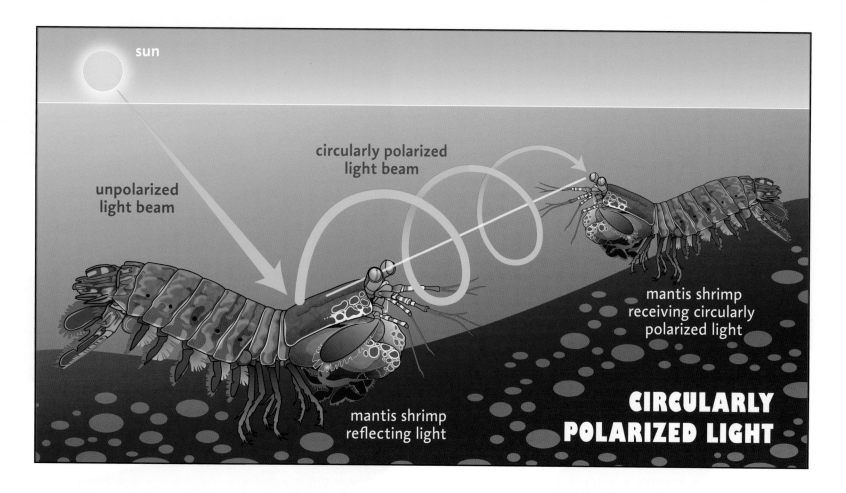

sun

unpolarized
light beam

circularly polarized
light beam

mantis shrimp
receiving circularly
polarized light

mantis shrimp
reflecting light

CIRCULARLY
POLARIZED LIGHT

Circularly polarized light is rare in nature. One of the few places you'll find it is shining off the bodies of stomatopods. When sunlight strikes a mantis shrimp, the light bounces off as spiral-shaped waves.

Mantis shrimps use this strange light bouncing off their bodies as a secret signal. A mantis shrimp can hide in a cranny in the coral and a predator won't be able to see it, but another mantis shrimp will. Gagnon discovered that if a mantis shrimp sees this unusual light shining out of a hole in the coral, it quickly retreats. It interprets the unusual glow as a sign that another mantis shrimp is hiding inside.

Gagnon thinks the stomatopods may use the light to actively communicate with one another. He explained that their tails give off stripes of circularly polarized light, and a mantis shrimp will sometimes lift its tail when it sees another of its kind. Are they threatening each other? Gagnon thinks so, although no one has tested this hypothesis. Based on his observations, he believes this tail-lifting behavior could be a secret signal, a way to say, "Hey look, I'm a stomatopod and you'd better watch out. I know you are one, I'm one too. Just walk away."

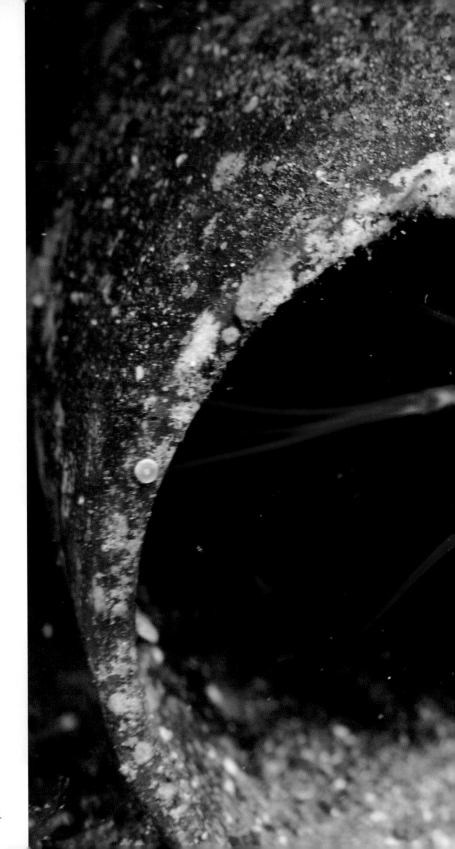

This mantis shrimp is keeping watch for intruders. Its powerful eyes can detect secret signals flashed by other stomatopods.

CHAPTER 3
Mighty Master of Smells

AFRICAN ELEPHANT
SCIENTIFIC NAME: *Loxodonta africana*
SECRET HIDEOUT: forests, shrublands, savannas, and deserts of sub-Saharan Africa
SIZE: up to 13 feet (4 m) tall at the shoulders
WEIGHT: up to 14,000 pounds (6,350 kg)
SECRET SENSE: supersensitive smell

In the hot savanna, a family of African elephants marches along a dirt road, trunks dangling above the dust. As the family tramps along, they sniff the ground. *Snuffle. Sniff.*

Suddenly, one elephant catches a whiff of something delicious. She goes into super-smell mode: trunk up! She takes a long inhale: *Sniiiiff!* Another elephant lifts her trunk, and another.

Soon all the elephants hold their trunks raised in the air. The whole family smells something tasty.

In one synchronous movement, they turn toward a distant grove of trees and pick up the pace in anticipation. Upon reaching the trees, they sniff around. *Olive trees?* Definitely not! *Mistletoe vine? That's it!* They can see the vines dangling from the top of the trees. They reach high and wrap their trunks around the vines. *Rustle! Snap!* They stuff big, leafy bunches of mistletoe into their mouths. *Yum!*

THE NOSE KNOWS

Elephants are massive mammals with immense appetites. An elephant must roam widely to find enough to eat. These huge herbivores can eat up to 300 pounds (136 kg) of food in a day! But they won't eat just anything. "They're like giant toddlers," said Melissa Schmitt. "They're incredibly picky."

Schmitt is an ecologist at the South African Environmental Observation Network. She wanted to know how these fussy eaters find their favorite foods. Do they use their eyes to scan the landscape for plants they like, the way you might size up the offerings at a buffet? Do they nibble as they go, using taste as a guide? Or does an elephant follow its humongous nose?

An elephant's trunk is the biggest nose in the animal world. Elephants treat their trunks like all-purpose tools. They use them to rub their eyes and pick up objects. They use them to stuff food or squirt water into their mouths. And they use them as big, movable odor detectors.

Melissa Schmitt works with semi-tame elephants that live in South Africa.

Schmitt wondered if an elephant used its supersensitive nose to sniff out food from far away. To find out, she had to do a little sleuthing. She followed elephants on the savanna and observed their eating habits. It isn't difficult to figure out what elephants like to eat. "They spit and slobber over everything," Schmitt said. Following the trail of elephant drool, she recorded which plants they ate and which ones they never touched.

Then Schmitt and her team gave the mighty mammals smell tests. They put different plants in two big garbage cans. One can contained a plant that elephants don't like, either olive or wild currant. The other held a favorite food, such as wild pear, bush willow, or their number one

Schmitt's team is testing whether this elephant can detect food by smell alone. The animal passed the test with flying colors!

The team discovered that elephants could even use their powerful noses to navigate a maze.

pick—mistletoe. Schmitt said elephants treat mistletoe as if it's the best dessert in the world. "It's like their chocolate cake," she said.

Once the cans were prepared, a handler brought an elephant to the cans and instructed the animal to choose which plant it wanted to eat. Lids with small holes covered the openings of the cans. The animal couldn't see what was inside the cans. It couldn't sneak its trunk in and touch the plant. It could only sniff the scent drifting through the holes. This task turned out to be easy for elephants.

By smell alone, they identified the plants they wanted to eat, even ones that smell the same to us.

Then Schmitt tested how well an elephant could sniff out food over longer distances. She and her team built an elephant-sized maze in the shape of a Y. Each arm of the Y led to a different plant. An elephant started at the bottom of the Y. It sniffed the air on each side and walked to the plant it chose. Again, elephants found this trick easy. Even over a long distance, they could track down their favorite foods by smell alone.

Schmitt's work has helped show that elephants can find food simply by pointing their trunks in the right direction and taking a big sniff. Other studies have shown that an elephant's trunk is packed with more odor receptors than any other animal has. These special nerve cells detect chemicals in the air and send that information to the olfactory bulb, the part of the brain that processes smells. The elephant has the largest known olfactory bulb on Earth.

Schmitt said when it comes to smells, an elephant's nose just knows. "You cannot fool elephants. You truly can't stump them."

Other research has shown elephants can smell mates, family members, and predators. They can recognize different tribes of people, distinguishing between a tribe that hunts them and another that leaves them alone. Their superb snouts can even sniff out and avoid land mines, explosive devices that are buried in the ground.

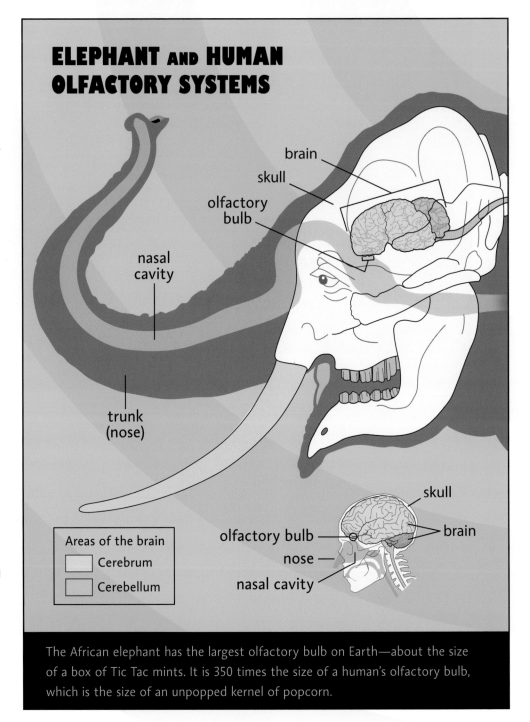

ELEPHANT AND HUMAN OLFACTORY SYSTEMS

brain

skull

olfactory bulb

nasal cavity

trunk (nose)

Areas of the brain
- Cerebrum
- Cerebellum

skull

olfactory bulb

brain

nose

nasal cavity

The African elephant has the largest olfactory bulb on Earth—about the size of a box of Tic Tac mints. It is 350 times the size of a human's olfactory bulb, which is the size of an unpopped kernel of popcorn.

Schmitt thinks people may be able to harness an elephant's superpower for another purpose: protecting the massive mammals. As elephants roam in search of food, they can run into danger. Poachers hunt them for their tusks. Farmers may kill elephants that trample their fields. What if people could spread bad odors in places that elephants should avoid? We could line the borders of farmers' fields or places where poachers roam to discourage elephants from walking there. Maybe those powerful noses could be used to help keep elephants safe.

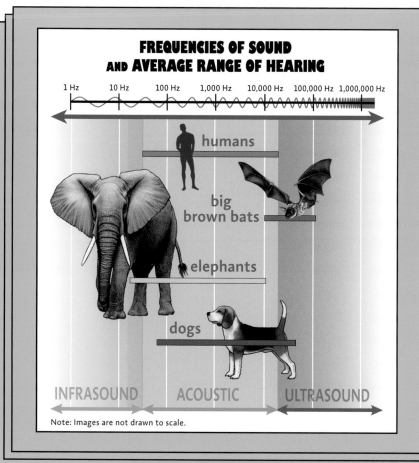

FREQUENCIES OF SOUND AND AVERAGE RANGE OF HEARING

1 Hz   10 Hz   100 Hz   1,000 Hz   10,000 Hz   100,000 Hz   1,000,000 Hz

humans

big brown bats

elephants

dogs

INFRASOUND   ACOUSTIC   ULTRASOUND

Note: Images are not drawn to scale.

SECRET SOUNDS

Elephants don't just have a great sense of smell—they also have extraordinary hearing. An African elephant's ears are the biggest on Earth—and some of the best. Elephants can communicate by making deep rumbles with their vocal cords. These rumbles, or infrasounds, are too low-pitched for our ears, but elephants can hear them just fine. Another elephant can hear the rumbles almost 6 miles (9.7 km) away. A distant elephant, too far off to hear the sound in the air, can still get the message. The rumbles carry through the ground for at least 10 to 20 miles (16 to 32 km). A far-off elephant can feel the vibrations with the special pads on its feet.

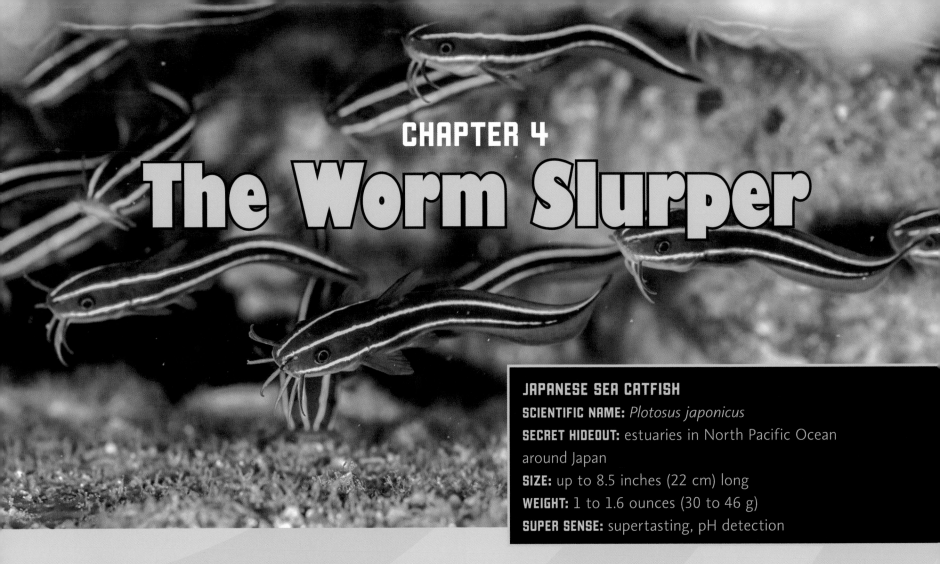

CHAPTER 4
The Worm Slurper

JAPANESE SEA CATFISH

SCIENTIFIC NAME: *Plotosus japonicus*
SECRET HIDEOUT: estuaries in North Pacific Ocean around Japan
SIZE: up to 8.5 inches (22 cm) long
WEIGHT: 1 to 1.6 ounces (30 to 46 g)
SUPER SENSE: supertasting, pH detection

A Japanese sea catfish cruises the muddy ocean floor. *Swiiish!* Its whiskers wave in the water. It is nighttime, and the ocean is dark.

Nearby, a bristle worm hides in its burrow in the mud. The catfish can't see the worm. And it can't smell the worm, because mud masks the worm's scent. The bristly creature stays still and doesn't disturb the water at all. There is nothing to give it away. Except for one thing: the worm needs to breathe.

As the catfish swims by, the worm lets out a tiny, worm-sized breath. *Pffff.* This releases a bubble of carbon dioxide into the water and changes the seawater near its burrow ever so slightly. The effect is small and fleeting, but it is enough.

The catfish's whiskers pick up the breath. *Aha!* The fish circles back and . . . *sluurrrrpp!* . . . sucks up the wriggling worm.

"SWIMMING TONGUES"

Biologist John Caprio studies the sense of taste in fish at Louisiana State University. Taste helps fish detect chemicals in the water. According to Caprio, catfish are the undisputed taste champions of the animal world.

"Catfish are swimming tongues," Caprio said. "There are taste buds all over their body."

You have taste buds clustered on your tongue. Look at your tongue in a mirror, and notice the bumps—each bump holds hundreds of taste buds. Altogether, you have somewhere between two thousand and eight thousand taste buds.

But a catfish might have as many as five hundred thousand taste buds, according to Caprio. Its body is smothered with them. Taste buds freckle the skin on its fins, back, sides, belly, and tail. They coat the whiskers that stick out of its face. Each one of those taste buds detects chemicals in the water. Nerves carry signals from the taste buds to the brain, telling a catfish when small fish or tasty worms are nearby.

Caprio was studying the Japanese sea catfish, a type of catfish that lives off the coast of Japan. He was testing how the whiskers of Japanese sea catfish respond to different tasting chemicals when he noticed something unexpected. The fish's supersensitive whiskers were detecting tiny changes in pH of the water itself.

In chemistry, pH is a measure of how basic or acidic a liquid is. Its range is 0 (very acidic) to 14 (very basic), with 7 as the neutral point. Seawater is slightly basic with an average pH of 8.2.

The ability to sense pH isn't unusual. For example, your body uses pH to control your breathing. If the pH of your blood drops too much, that's a sign that you have too much carbon dioxide in

UNDERWATER SUPER SNIFFERS

Nearly three thousand species of catfish live in streams, lakes, rivers, and oceans around the world. Although catfish can see, most hunt in muddy, murky waters where sight is not much use. So they track down dinner by tasting the water with their skin and whiskers, or barbels. Catfish also have powerful nostrils that can sniff out chemicals in the water. A catfish's nose is so incredible that it can smell one molecule of a chemical floating in ten billion molecules of water!

your blood. When that happens, sensors in your brain tell you to take in a breath.

But Japanese sea catfish are remarkable because they have pH sensors on the outside—not the inside—of their bodies. Caprio wondered why. After all, the pH of seawater doesn't really change; it stays a constant 8.2. "Why would nature build such a highly sensitive pH-sensing system in a fish?" he wondered. "It made no sense." Even more puzzling, the changes the fish picks up are teensy—less than a tenth of a pH unit. Caprio was determined to learn why these swimming tongues would need yet another supersensory ability.

He discovered that pH-sensing turns the Japanese sea catfish into fearsome worm-slurping machines. Bristle worms are a favorite food of the Japanese sea catfish. The prickly worms hide in tube-shaped burrows they dig in the mud.

"As long as the worm is quiet and isn't moving around, the fish can't detect it normally," said Caprio. "But what the worm has to do is breathe."

This gives it away. As worms give off tiny exhalations, they release carbon dioxide gas into the water. The gas reacts with water and forms an acid, which turns the water near the entrances to their burrows slightly more acidic for

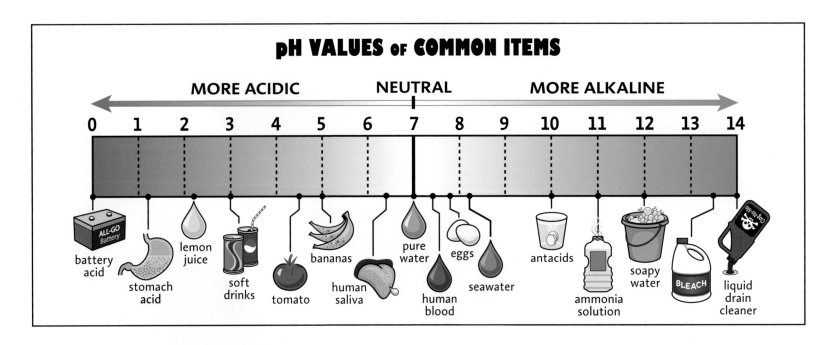

pH VALUES OF COMMON ITEMS

MORE ACIDIC   NEUTRAL   MORE ALKALINE

0   1   2   3   4   5   6   7   8   9   10   11   12   13   14

battery acid
stomach acid
lemon juice
soft drinks
tomato
bananas
human saliva
pure water
human blood
eggs
seawater
antacids
ammonia solution
soapy water
BLEACH
liquid drain cleaner

just a moment. By sensing this drop in pH with its whiskers, the catfish can zero in on hidden worms.

Caprio placed sea catfish in tanks with buried bristle worms. He set up infrared cameras to capture images and video footage in the dark, and turned off the light to watch them hunt. Even in pitch-black tanks, the catfish quickly found the worms. Then he removed the remaining worms and pumped tiny amounts of slightly more acidic water out of a tube in the bottom of the tank. The catfish swam around the tube, biting it. The fish was reading the tiny shift in pH as a sign that a worm was inside.

Caprio wonders if other catfish and maybe even other kinds of fish have this ability. "Of over 30,000 species of fish, this is the only species that we know is a pH sensor," Caprio said. It's possible other fish could have it too, he said, though he doesn't know because no one has looked yet.

A wriggling bristle worm is a tempting target for a Japanese sea catfish. Even if the worm hides, the catfish can still detect it.

Japanese sea catfish hunt for prey in schools, using their supersensitive whiskers to find hidden worms.

CHAPTER 5
Seeing with Sound

BIG BROWN BAT
SCIENTIFIC NAME: *Eptesicus fuscus*
SECRET HIDEOUT: forests, meadows, deserts, farms, and cities in North America, Central America, and northern South America
SIZE: wingspan up to 16 inches (41 cm)
WEIGHT: up to 0.8 ounces (23 g)
SECRET SENSES: ultrasonic hearing, echolocation

In a woodland glade, the sun sinks lower . . . lower . . . and out of sight. Darkness descends.

A hungry big brown bat flies around the clearing and screams out a series of chirps: *CHREEP–CHREEP–CHREEP*. In a blink, the sound bounces back: *chroop–chroop–chroop*. The bat hears a picture of everything in its path. *Swish!* It swerves around a tree.

As the bat circles, a moth enters the clearing. *Flit-flit*. It heads for a nearby tree, flying for safety.

The bat keeps chirping. *CHREEP–CHREEP–CHREEP*. It hears the soft echo bouncing off the moth. *Chrooff–chrooff–chrooff*.

Swoop! The bat turns and speeds toward the moth, its chirps coming faster and faster. *CHREEPCHREEPCHREEEEEEEE!* The bat opens its mouth wide. *Chomp!* It crunches the unlucky insect to bits.

TO THE BAT LAB!

When you see bats flying around at night, they might seem silent, but they are making ultrasonic sounds, chirps too high for your ears to hear. "Even though we can't hear [bats], they're actually very loud in their calls," said Te Jones.

She is part of a team led by Cynthia Moss at Johns Hopkins University. The team studies bat echolocation. Jones explained that as bats fly, they emit a beam of sound from their mouth or nose. A bat can aim the beam in different directions, the way you might move your eyes to look at something. Jones calls this the bat's "acoustic gaze." Objects in the center of the sound beam produce the strongest echoes, while objects to the side produce weaker echoes. If an insect flies through the beam of sound, a bat has the extraordinary ability to tell the insect's size, location, speed of flight, and direction. As a bat closes in on its prey, its chirps come faster and faster and turn into a whirr, or a feeding buzz.

Jones and her coworkers are trying to learn how these masters of sound build mental pictures from echoes. They use the Bat Lab, a dark room lined with highly sensitive microphones and cameras that can record images in the dark. In another room, behind a sign that reads Bat Crossing, big brown bats nestle together.

Jones brings the bats into the Bat Lab and trains them to do tricks. "They're very smart," she said. She can train a bat to fly around the room in the dark and

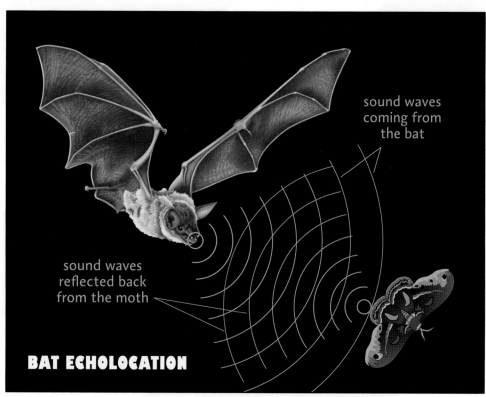

sound waves coming from the bat

sound waves reflected back from the moth

BAT ECHOLOCATION

echolocate to find a juicy mealworm dangling from a string. Every time the bat performs the trick correctly, she rewards it with a treat. But not all bats cooperate. "They each have their own individual personalities," she said. "It's kind of like training a cat."

Once the training is complete, the experiments can begin. The bat wears a tiny, bat-sized headset so Jones can record its superpowered brain waves. As the furry mammal performs its task, the headset records its brain activity. Microphones in the room pick up its calls, and cameras record its flight path. By comparing brain waves, calls, and movements, Jones can assemble a picture of what this small superhero is experiencing.

She is testing how these amazing animals cope with background noise, because outside the Bat Lab, the real world is noisy. As a bat swoops and swerves, using its ultrasonic ears to find insects,

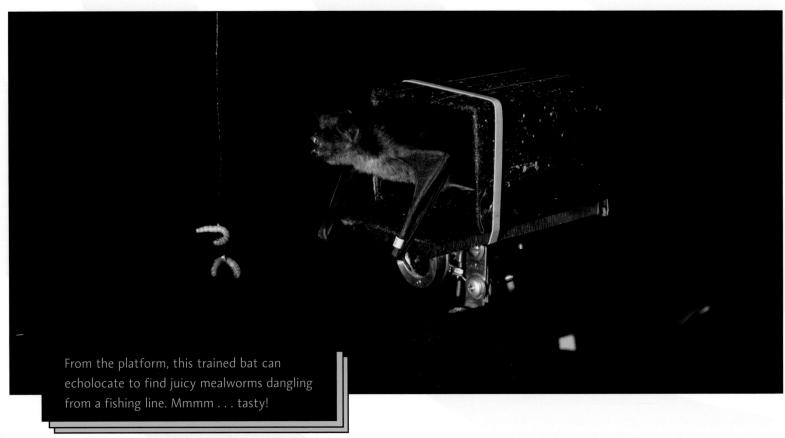

From the platform, this trained bat can echolocate to find juicy mealworms dangling from a fishing line. Mmmm . . . tasty!

it might also be calling to other bats. Other bats are calling too. And all those echoes are bouncing off bushes, trees, insects, and one another. Jones compares it to trying to listen at a loud party. "Everyone is chatting and you're trying to talk to one specific person," she said. "What tends to happen is you speak with a higher volume and you enunciate more. You might repeat yourself to make sure someone has heard you."

She has found that bats make similar adjustments. In her experiments, bats echolocate while she broadcasts recorded bat calls in the background. She has discovered that bats adjust their calls so they can hear themselves. They call a little louder. They change the pitch and stretch out the duration of their chirps.

Jones and other members of the Bat Lab are still learning how bats filter out the noise and adjust their calls so they can hear themselves in a loud environment. Their work is filling in the details of how these masterful mammals can paint a picture of the world with sound—even when the world gets a little noisy.

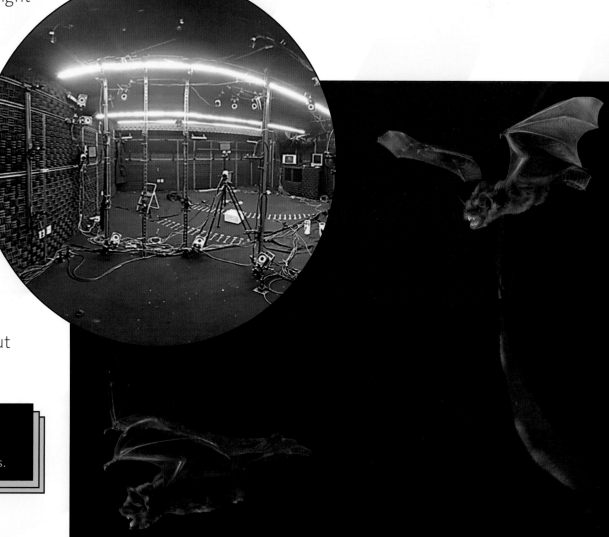

Jones tests how bats navigate with sound in the Bat Lab, a room outfitted with microphones and infrared cameras.

CHAPTER 6

Night Vision

SIDEWINDER RATTLESNAKE

SCIENTIFIC NAME: *Crotalus cerastes*

SECRET HIDEOUT: deserts in the southwestern United States and northwestern Mexico

SIZE: up to 32 inches (82 cm) long

WEIGHT: up to 10.7 ounces (304 g)

SECRET SENSE: heat sensing or infrared vision

It is night in the Mojave Desert. Under the dark sky, a sidewinder rattlesnake slithers across the loose sand, seeking a place to hunt.

The snake selects a spot near some bushes. It coils up on the sand, its body cocked and ready. The snake watches the bushes and waits.

Something is stirring. *Hop!* A kangaroo rat pops out of the brush. It does not notice the snake.

But to the snake, the warm rat shines brightly.

When the rat moves again—*hop!*—the snake strikes. *Attack!*

Surprised in midjump, the rat twists in the air, trying to escape. But the snake is a heat-seeking missile. *Chomp!* It bites down, and venom flows into its prey. In moments, the venom will take effect and the rattlesnake will eat.

SEE LIKE A SNAKE

When a sidewinder rattlesnake hunts, it coils on the ground at night, stays still, and waits for unsuspecting rodents and birds to wander within striking distance. Once prey comes near, heat vision guides its strike.

A rattlesnake is a pit viper. It's called that because of its two holes, or pits, that sit on either side of its head between its eyes and nostrils. The pits are superpowered sensory organs that detect infrared light given off by warm objects.

Infrared light is another type of light that's invisible to our eyes, but we can feel it as heat. Rattlesnakes can see it. It's their secret weapon. The body of a warm-blooded animal radiates waves of infrared light. If a warm animal passes in front of a rattler, the radiation enters the pit organs. Nerves in the pits pass that signal to the visual center of a snake's brain.

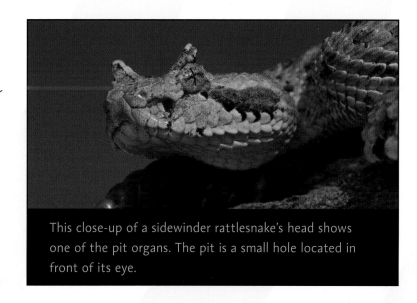

This close-up of a sidewinder rattlesnake's head shows one of the pit organs. The pit is a small hole located in front of its eye.

ELECTROMAGNETIC SPECTRUM

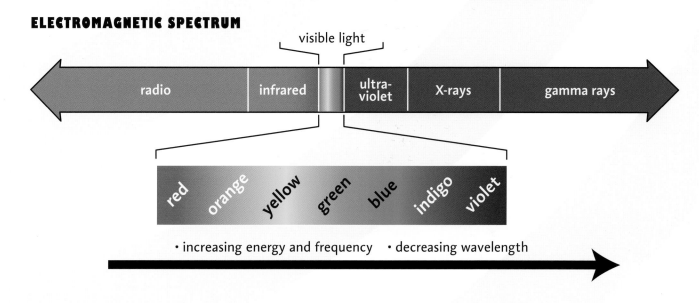

visible light

radio | infrared | ultra-violet | X-rays | gamma rays

red orange yellow green blue indigo violet

• increasing energy and frequency   • decreasing wavelength

"The image is probably quite blurry," said Hannes Schraft, a biologist at the University of Quebec. He has studied how heat sensing works in rattlesnakes. The snake's brain overlays the blurry image from the pits on top of the clearer image from the eyes. To a rattlesnake, a warm kangaroo rat likely gleams like a glow stick in the night.

Schraft has studied how rattlesnakes use their heat-sensing superpower to hunt. "They can detect contrasts, or differences, quite well," he said. So a warm rat in the cool night really stands out. That's the same way a black dot against a white background stands out to you.

Schraft wondered whether snakes use their heat-sensing pits to help them find their way at night. Do they navigate with their super-sensing pits, their eyes, or both? To find out, he had to come up with a way to block the snake's vision or its pit organs. "You have to devise a way to ask an animal what it perceives," he explained.

First, he had to coax a rattlesnake into a tube, which made the venomous animal safe to handle. Then he gave the snake a drug that put it to sleep. He blindfolded some rattlers with duct tape. "It doesn't hurt the snake because a snake's eye is covered with a transparent scale," Schraft said. He used tweezers to plug the pit organs of other snakes with tiny balls of beeswax. In some snakes he covered the eyes and plugged the pit organs.

Once the snakes were awake, he released each one into a fenced-off arena with a few bushes to see how well the animal could find its way around. Snakes with plugged pits navigated the arena just fine. But blindfolded snakes couldn't find their way, whether or not their pit organs were blocked.

This image, taken with an infrared camera, shows what a rattlesnake might see when it looks at a Merriam's kangaroo rat. The rats are a favorite food of sidewinder rattlesnakes.

The result surprised him. "We thought they would use the pit organs to find bushes," he said, "because bushes are warmer compared to the cool sand at night. But they don't." His experiment showed that vision is the way a snake navigates. Heat sensing, it turns out, is a superpower reserved for snagging a midnight snack.

Schraft calls it "mind-boggling" to study an animal with such an unusual sensory system. "As humans we think we know everything there is to know through our senses. But really there's so much more out there."

On a dark night outside of Yuma, Arizona, Schraft tests how a rattlesnake uses heat to hunt a kangaroo rat.

TALENTED TONGUE

A rattlesnake may use heat vision to strike prey in total darkness, but first it tracks down the prey with its forked tongue. When a rattlesnake is hunting, it flicks out its tongue repeatedly. With each flick, scent molecules from the air stick to its tongue. Between flicks, the snake touches the tips of its tongue to the roof of its mouth. The Jacobson's organ, a special sense organ, transmits a scent signal to the snake's brain. The snake can track down its prey by sensing whether the smell is stronger to its left or to its right.

Track and Attack

An electric eel slips through the slow current of a lazy river. Night has fallen, and the eel is hungry. Prey is impossible to spot in these dark, murky waters. How can the eel find its next meal?

Zzzzipp! As it swims, the eel creates an electric field around itself, like a bubble. The eel passes a bed of kelp, and this creates a ripple in the electric field—*zzzzopp!*—which the eel feels on its skin. A fish is hiding in the kelp, staying motionless to avoid detection by predators.

But the eel knows the kelp is a good hiding spot. To flush out any hidden prey, the eel aims two quick blasts of electricity—*zip! zoop!*—into the kelp. The charge passes through the fish's body and causes it to jerk violently. This sends a ripple through the water. It alerts the eel to the fish's location.

The eel attacks. It fires more electrical blasts at the fish. *Zap-zap-zap!* The attack is so powerful that the fish freezes in place, its muscles disabled. The eel lunges, mouth open. Fresh fish for dinner.

TRACK AND ATTACK

Despite their name, an electric eel isn't a true eel. It is a type of knife fish, more closely related to catfish and carp. An electric eel is a nocturnal hunter that finds food with electricity.

"Eels are essentially batteries immersed in water," said Ken Catania, a neuroscientist at Vanderbilt University in Tennessee. He has studied how electric eels use electricity to hunt.

An electric eel's body is packed with electrocytes. These supercharged cells run in rows along the length of the eel's body. Electrocytes store and produce electricity. By firing these cells together, an electric eel can create either weak electric pulses or a strong electric blast.

The electric eel generates electric shocks using special cells called electrocytes.

Electric eels use their weak pulses like radar. As an eel swims, the electric field around its body helps it navigate the dark waters. Distortions in the field reveal a nearby object's size, shape, and distance. The supersensitive eel feels these objects as electric images on its skin. The eel can even tell whether the object is alive, since a living animal conducts electricity, while a rock does not.

Pits dot an electric eel's body. The pits are packed with electroreceptors, cells that can sense electricity.

Their ability to sense electricity is a superpower called electroreception. This sixth sense comes from electroreceptors. These special cells sense changes in the electric field. They are grouped together in pits, which speckle the eel's body.

An eel's strong electric blast is a terrifying superweapon, one the animal is famous for. Its zap can be as high as 860 volts, enough to easily knock down a horse. Catania has discovered that the eel uses its strong electric blast as both a weapon and a supersensory system. By tricking electric eels into attacking in the lab and recording these attacks with high-speed cameras, he has pieced together how this happens.

If a fish is hiding out of reach of the eel's weak electric radar, the predator can still flush it out. It can fire off two quick electric pulses. This doublet causes the muscles of any nearby fish to give a big twitch. The eel feels by touch the ripples this movement sends through the water.

The eel then fires its weapon—rapid, high-voltage blasts, up to four hundred per second—at its prey. These blasts disable the muscles of the fish temporarily so it can't swim away.

But the eel must continue to track the fish so it knows where to bite down. The ripples only give the eel a general idea of the fish's location, and a paralyzed fish could drift away in the current. And so, as the eel attacks, it tracks the location of its paralyzed prey with its superpowered electroreceptors. Even if the paralyzed fish drifts, the eel can follow it in the dark.

Eels can also discharge their weapons against bigger living things that they consider a threat. If people or horses wade into their territory, eels can deliver a *zoop-zoop-zoop* to the leg. Although the attack itself isn't fatal, it does cause terrible pain and can cause the victim to drown.

Many mysteries remain about electric eels, such as how an eel carries out its attack in the wild and how it avoids shocking its own nervous system with its high-voltage blasts. Catania used to think electric eels were primitive creatures. Now that he knows what they can do, he regards the eel as "one of the most sophisticated predators out there."

The eel stuns its prey with a strong electric blast. Then it tracks the stunned prey using its super electric sensing.

CHAPTER 8
The Magnetic Missile

RED FOX

SCIENTIFIC NAME: *Vulpes vulpes*

SECRET HIDEOUT: forests, grasslands, mountains, and deserts in North America, Europe, Asia, and North Africa

SIZE: up to 57 inches (146 cm) from the nose to the tip of the tail

WEIGHT: up to 31 pounds (14 kg)

SUPER SENSE: magnetoreception

It's winter, and a red fox trots across a snow-covered meadow. The only sound is the *phooof* of her breath and the *pit-pit-pit* of her furry feet on thick snow.

The fox hears something. She stops. Tilts her head. Listens.

Scritch-scritch-scritch.

The sound is a field mouse—fox food—stirring under the snow. She cannot see the mouse. But she still has a way to pinpoint its location.

Scritch-scritch.

There it is again. The fox listens and takes aim. Her body is pointing northeast, which is no accident.

Scritch-scritch-scritch.

LEAP! The fox arcs high into the wintry air, shifts her tail slightly in midleap, and—*PLUNGE!*— dives headfirst into the snow. Head and front paws disappear under the icy cover. Seconds later, the fox emerges, face coated with snow and a mouse in her jaws.

TARGET PRACTICE

A red fox can hear mice, voles, and other small rodents through thick snow cover. Like a guided missile, the fox can leap high and drop with deadly accuracy on its target—all without seeing what it's about to eat. This impressive hunting move is called mousing.

When scientists in the Czech Republic studied mousing leaps, they noticed something odd. The researchers had tramped into fields and watched red foxes hunt. They had taken careful note of the place, time, season, and weather conditions of over eight hundred mousing leaps. And they measured one other thing: the direction of each jump.

The scientists discovered that when foxes hunt in snow or thick brush—when they can't see their prey—they prefer to jump in a northeasterly direction. To be exact, the direction is 20 degrees off from magnetic north (the "N" on a compass). When foxes leaped in that direction, they had good aim, catching most of their prey. But if they leapt in other directions, they almost always missed.

So, what's going on?

A red fox mouses in wintertime. It can leap and land precisely on a mouse without ever seeing its target.

"There's no doubt these animals are able to sense the magnetic field," said Michael Painter, a biologist at Barry University in Florida.

Earth has a magnetic field around it. Magnetoreception (mag-NEE-toe-ree-SEP-shun) is the ability to sense the field. Many animals can sense our planet's magnetic field. Birds use it as a compass when they migrate, and sea turtles use it to find their birthplace to lay eggs. Cattle and roe deer tend to align their bodies in a north-south direction when resting or grazing. But a red fox is the first animal known to use it to hunt.

How would sensing the magnetic field help a fox land on its lunch? Painter thinks it helps a fox judge the distance to its target. He has a hunch a fox sees the magnetic field with its eyes, but he can't prove it yet. Here's how seeing the field might help a fox take aim.

Imagine you have a flashlight strapped to your waist. Suppose the flashlight aims down at an angle, so you always see a spot of light exactly 5 feet (1.5 m) away. Imagine that's how the fox sees the magnetic field, a spot of light that's always the same distance ahead of it. When hunting hidden prey, the fox creeps forward until the light lines up with the location of the sound. Then it leaps and lands with pinpoint accuracy.

NOW HEAR THIS

A red fox has big, triangle-shaped ears for detecting prey. The shape catches and funnels sounds into the ear canal. A fox can move each ear independently as it rotates its ears toward the source of a sound. The ears are supersensitive to low-pitched sounds that we can't hear—like the soft sound of tiny footsteps under the snow. Because the ears are spaced far apart, the sound arrives at each ear at a slightly different time. A fox learns to use this delay to pinpoint the location of the sound before pouncing.

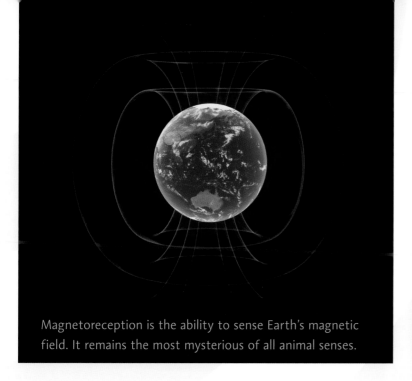

Magnetoreception is the ability to sense Earth's magnetic field. It remains the most mysterious of all animal senses.

This semi-tame fox wears a collar that tracks its movements as well as the direction it is facing.

But the fox has to be facing the right direction to sense the field. If it faces the wrong direction, it must rely solely on sound. It listens, it creeps, it leaps—but it misses its prey most of the time.

Painter is working with the Czech teams to follow up on their findings. He's using special tracking collars that can record what the fox is doing—whether it is sleeping, walking, or jumping—and which direction it is facing at the time. He's tested the collars on semi-tame foxes and will try them on wild foxes next.

He can even use the collars to turn off the fox's magnetic sense. The collars can emit radio waves, which interfere with magnetoreception. Painter hopes in the future to use the collars to shut down a fox's magnetic sensing for short times. With the collars, he could run controlled experiments. He could turn off the magnetic sense in one group of foxes while leaving magnetic sensing on in a control group. Then he could compare how a fox's behavior changes when it can or can't detect the field.

Painter admits that magnetoreception is tough to study because scientists know so little about it. "It's sometimes frustrating that there's all these questions we don't have answers to," he said. "But it also makes it pretty exciting and fun."

Making Sense of Animal Senses

f you could have an animal's superpowered sense, what would it be? A rattlesnake's night vision? A mantis shrimp's skill with secret messages? A bat's ability to see with sound?

When it comes to animal senses, nature has no shortage of creative strategies. But why do some animals have such sensational abilities?

n any population of animals, some ndividuals have traits that give them an advantage for survival. A keen sense can be a big advantage. An animal that possesses t may be able to live longer and produce more offspring. If the animal's offspring inherit the heightened sense, they too may enjoy an edge in survival. n this way, sharp senses can be passed on and refined from generation to generation. Over long periods, extraordinary senses can evolve.

The powerful sense always matches an animal's lifestyle. A rattlesnake has heat vision. It's perfect for a nocturnal hunter of warm-blooded mammals. An electric eel has electroreception, ideal for finding prey hiding in dark and murky waters.

Heat vision gives this nocturnal hunter a unique survival advantage.

Scientists use the German word umwelt (OOM-velt) to describe an animal's sensory world, its unique way of perceiving and responding to its environment. Umwelt is what makes the study of sensory biology so challenging. We human beings have our *own* umwelt, our own sensory world. So it can be difficult to imagine a sensory experience that is so different from our own.

But scientists have found innovative ways to unlock the mysteries of animal senses. Sometimes they carefully observe how an animal acts, such as noticing that a fox points its body in a certain direction when it hunts. Other times they give an animal a test, such as testing whether an elephant can sniff out its favorite food. Or they might study animal bodies and brains, like counting the nerve fibers in a star-nosed mole's snout or counting the odor receptors that line an elephant's trunk.

An African elephant has more odor receptors than any other animal.

People have studied animal senses for a long time. Even so, many mysteries remain. How many different kinds of fish can sense pH? Could an elephant's sense of smell be used to protect the majestic beasts? How does an electric eel avoid knocking itself out with its electric shock? Those mysteries are waiting for future scientists to solve them. Maybe that future scientist could be you. What if the next big breakthrough in animal super senses was your own?

AUTHOR'S NOTE

The idea that sparked this book came in 2007 when I was assigned to write a magazine article about the way birds use Earth's magnetic field as a compass. I was intrigued that animals can sense things that are hidden from us. We humans tend to think the way we sense the world *is* the world. But there is more to it than that. I began to think of extraordinary animal senses as a kind of superpower. I wondered, What else can animals sense that we can't? And if we can't sense the same thing ourselves and we can't ask animals what they sense, how do we learn about those senses? These were the questions that drove this book.

I want to thank the scientists who helped make this book possible. Talking with them about their work was a highlight of my research. Thank you to John Caprio of Louisiana State University, Yakir Gagnon of Lund University in Sweden, Te Jones of Johns Hopkins University in Maryland, Duncan Leitch of the University of British Columbia in Canada, Michael Painter of Barry University in Florida, Melissa Schmitt of the South African Environmental Observation Network, and Hannes Schraft of Quebec University in Canada. I was inspired listening to their stories of how they conceived and carried out their experiments. I loved hearing what made the work both challenging and exciting, and what mysteries are still waiting to be solved.

GLOSSARY

acidic: having the chemical characteristic of an acid, a substance that tastes sour, can react with a base to form a salt, and can turn blue litmus paper red. Vinegar is a type of acid.

basic: having the chemical characteristic of a base. A base is a substance that tastes bitter, can react with an acid to form a salt, and can turn litmus paper blue. Ammonia is an example of a base.

biologist: a scientist who studies living things

carbon dioxide: a colorless, odorless gas made of carbon and oxygen. People and animals breathe this gas out.

conduct: to allow electricity to pass through

echolocation: a radarlike way that bats (and other animals including whales) locate distant objects by producing sound waves and listening to the echoes reflected from the objects

ecologist: a scientist who studies the relationship between living things and their environment

electric field: a region around a charged particle or charged object

electricity: a form of energy caused by the movement of negatively charged particles, or electrons

electrocyte: a specialized cell that generates electricity

electroreception: a sense that allows a living thing to detect electric fields or currents

electroreceptor: an organ or sensory cell that can detect electric fields

estuary: a body of water found where a river meets the sea

evolve: to change gradually over time

habitat: the place where an animal or plant naturally lives

herbivore: an animal that eats plants

infrared light: a type of light that cannot be seen by the human eye. Infrared light lies outside the visible spectrum at the red end and is given off by warm objects.

infrasound: sounds that are too low-pitched to be heard by the human ear

magnetic field: a region around a magnet or other magnetic body, such as Earth, within which magnetic forces can be detected

magnetoreception: a sense that allows a living thing to detect a magnetic field

mammal: a warm-blooded animal with fur that makes milk for its babies

migrate: to move from one place to another when the seasons change

molecule: the smallest particle of a chemical substance

nerve: a band of tissue that sends messages between the brain and other organs, such as sensory organs

nerve fiber: a threadlike part of a cell. Nerve fibers bundled together form nerves.

neuroscientist: a scientist who studies the nervous system

nocturnal: active at night

pH: a measure of how acidic or basic a substance is. Acids have a pH greater than 7, and bases have a pH less than 7. A substance with a pH of 7 is neutral.

poacher: a person who hunts or fishes illegally

predator: an animal that eats other animals for food

prey: an animal eaten by a predator

rodent: a member of a group of mammals that includes mice, beavers, and squirrels. All rodents have large, sharp front teeth that are used for gnawing.

savanna: a grassland in Africa containing scattered trees

species: a category of living things that is able to produce offspring

subterranean: living under Earth's surface

taste bud: sense organs that recognize taste

ultrasound: sounds that are too high-pitched to be heard by the human ear

ultraviolet light: a type of light that cannot be seen by the human eye. Ultraviolet light lies past the violet-colored end of the visible light spectrum.

SOURCE NOTES

9 Duncan Leitch, phone call with the author, April 1, 2020.

9 Leitch.

9 Leitch.

13 Yakir Luc Gagnon, Skype call with the author, May 4, 2020.

14 Gagnon.

17 Melissa H. Schmitt, Skype call with the author, April 9, 2020.

18 Schmitt.

19 Schmitt.

20 Schmitt.

23 John Caprio, phone call with the author, May 14, 2020.

24 Caprio.

24 Caprio.

25 Caprio.

27 Te K. Jones, Skype call with the author, March 16, 2020.

27 Jones.

28 Jones.

29 Jones.

32 Hannes Schraft, Skype call with the author, March 10, 2020.

32 Schraft.

32 Schraft.

32 Schraft.

33 Schraft.

33 Schraft.

35 Heidi Hall, "Biologist Reaches into Electric Eel Tank, Comes Out with Equation to Measure Shocks," Vanderbilt University, September 14, 2017, https://news.vanderbilt.edu/2017/09/14/biologist-reaches-into-electric-eel-tank-comes-out-with-equation-to-measure-shocks/.

37 Jason Bittel, "The Electric Eel's Superpower Just Got Even Cooler," *National Geographic*, October 20, 2015, https://www.nationalgeographic.com/news/2015/10/151020-electric-eel-evolution-high-voltage-sensory-weapon-animals-science/.

40 Michael Painter, phone call with the author, March 12, 2020.

41 Painter.

SELECTED BIBLIOGRAPHY

You can find the complete bibliography of sources I consulted at http://rebeccahirsch.com/sensational-senses.com.

Caprio, John, Mami Shimohara, Takayuki Marui, Shuitsu Harada, and Sadao Kiyohara. "Marine Teleost Locates Live Prey through Ph Sensing." *Science* 344, no. 6188 (2014): 1154–1156.

Catania, Kenneth C. "The Astonishing Behavior of Electric Eels." *Frontiers in Integrative Neuroscience* 13, no. 23 (July 16, 2019): 1–18.

Červený, Jaroslav, Sabine Begall, Petr Koubek, Petra Nováková, and Hynek Burda. "Directional Preference May Enhance Hunting Accuracy in Foraging Foxes." *Biology Letters* 7, no. 3 (May 2011): 355–357.

Gagnon, Yakir Luc, Rachel Marie Templin, Martin John How, and N. Justin Marshall. "Circularly Polarized Light as a Communication Signal in Mantis Shrimps." *Current Biology* 25 (December 7, 2015): 3074–3078.

Jones, Te K., Melville J. Wohlgemuth, and William E. Conner. "Active Acoustic Interference Elicits Echolocation Changes in Heterospecific Bats." *Journal of Experimental Biology* 221 (August 13, 2018): 1–7.

Leitch, Duncan B., Diana K. Sarko, and Kenneth C. Catania. "Brain Mass and Cranial Nerve Size in Shrews and Moles." *Scientific Reports* 4, no. 6241 (September 1, 2014): 1–7.

Painter, Michael S., Justin A. Blanco, E. Pascal Malkemper, Chris Anderson, Daniel C. Sweeney, Charles W. Hewgle, Jaroslav Červený et al. "Use of Bio-Loggers to Characterize Red Fox Behavior with Implications for Studies of Magnetic Alignment Responses in Free-Roaming Animals." *Animal Biotelemetry* 4, no. 20 (November 15, 2016): 1–19.

Schmitt, Melissa H., Adam Shuttleworth, David Ward, and Adrian M. Shrader. "African Elephants Use Plant Odours to Make Foraging Decisions across Multiple Spatial Scales." *Animal Behaviour* 141 (May 2018): 17–27.

Schraft, Hannes A., and Rulon W. Clark. "Sensory Basis of Navigation in Snakes: The Relative Importance of Eyes and Pit Organs." *Animal Behaviour* 147 (January 2019): 77–82.

MORE TO EXPLORE

BOOKS

Castaldo, Nancy. *Beastly Brains: Exploring How Animals Think, Talk, and Feel*. New York: Houghton Mifflin Harcourt, 2017.
Learn about the world of animal brains and what life is like for different animals.

Duprat, Guillaume. *Eye Spy: Wild Ways Animals See the World*. Greenbelt, MD: What on Earth Books, 2018.
Learn how eyes work, and see the many ways animals view the world around them.

Figueras, Emmanuelle. *Nose Knows: Wild Ways Animals Smell the World*. Greenbelt, MD: What on Earth Books, 2019.
Discover how smell plays a key role in the lives of different animals and shapes their behavior.

Newman, Patricia. *Eavesdropping on Elephants: How Listening Helps Conservation*. Minneapolis: Millbrook Press, 2018.
This book delves into new discoveries scientists are making about how elephants communicate using sound.

MOVIES

"Fox Dives Headfirst into Snow"
https://www.youtube.com/watch?v=D2SoGHFM18I
This video of a red fox doing mousing leaps in thick snow will help you appreciate just how good it is at using Earth's magnetic field to target its prey.

"Marine Teleost Locates Live Prey through pH Sensing"
https://science.sciencemag.org/content/suppl/2014/06 /04/344.6188.1154.DC1
See a Japanese sea catfish swim out of its nest, locate a polychaete worm, and slurp it down.

"The Snail-Smashing, Fish-Spearing, Eye-Popping Mantis Shrimp"
https://www.youtube.com/watch?v=Lm1ChtK9QDU
Learn more about how a mantis shrimp's punch goes hand in hand with its extraordinary eyesight.

"Star-Nosed Mole High-Speed Behavior"
https://static-content.springer.com/esm /art%3A10.1038%2Fnature03250/MediaObjects /41586_2005_BFnature03250_MOESM5_ESM.mov
This brief video clip shows why a star-nosed mole is in the *Guinness World Records* as the fastest-eating mammal.

"Steering by Hearing"
https://batlab.johnshopkins.edu/pages/movies /steeringbyhearing.mp4
You can listen in as a big brown bat uses echolocation while flying outdoors. You can also see how a big brown bat in the Bat Lab aimed its sound beam in different directions and zeroed in on its prey with a feeding buzz.

"Strange, Surprising and Star-Nosed"
https://www.youtube.com/watch?v=UMz0Q7VbT9w
Watch a brief video clip of a star-nosed mole doing underwater sniffing.

WEBSITES

Adventures with Elephants
https://adventureswithelephants.com/our-elephants
Meet the elephants at the Adventures with Elephants facility near Bela Bela, Limpopo Province, South Africa, where Melissa Schmitt did her research.

Echolocation, National Park Service
https://www.nps.gov/subjects/bats/echolocation.htm
Listen to bat echolocation calls slowed down so you can hear them. The calls of the spotted bat are faintly audible to people with good ears. Test your ears. Can you hear the spotted bat?

INDEX

PHOTO ACKNOWLEDGMENTS

Image credits: Nikhil Patil/Getty Images, p. 4; Westend61/Getty Images, p. 5 (bottom); Courtesy of the Moss Lab, p. 5 (top); Stan Tekiela Author/Naturalist/Wildlife Photographer/Getty Images, p. 6; All Canada Photos/Alamy Stock Photo, p. 7; myrrha/Getty Images, p. 8 (left); © 2011 Catania et al. (public domain), p. 8 (right); © Dwight Kuhn, p. 9; Steve Jones/Alamy Stock Photo, p. 10; Alex Permiakov/Shutterstock.com, p. 11; Beverly Speed/Shutterstock.com, p. 12; Zainal Amar Zainal Abidin/Shutterstock.com, pp. 14–15; phototrip/Alamy Stock Photo, p. 16; © Melissa Schmitt, pp. 17, 18, 19; LITTLE DINOSAUR/Alamy Stock Photo, p. 22; Pete Niesen/Alamy Stock Photo, p. 25 (right); Anilao Villa Magdalena/Shutterstock.com, p. 25 (left); robertharding/Alamy Stock Photo, p. 26; © Brock Fenton and Benjamin Falk/JHU BatLab, pp. 28, 29 (left); JHU BatLab, p. 29 (right); Alexander Wong/iStock/Getty Images, p. 30; John Cancalosi/Alamy Stock Photo, p. 31 (top); © Hannes Schraft, pp. 32, 33 (top); Mark_Kostich/Shutterstock.com, p. 33 (bottom); Kseniia Mnasina/Shutterstock.com, p. 34; Pally/Alamy Stock Photo, pp. 35, 37; stacey_newman/iStock/Getty Images, p. 36; OliverChilds/Getty Images, p. 38; John Conrad/Getty Images, p. 39; Scott Suriano/Getty Images, p. 40; Science Photo Library/ANDRZEJ WOJCICKI/Getty Images, p. 41 (left); © Mike Painter, p. 41 (right); Mlorenzphotography/Getty Images, p. 42; StuPorts/Getty Images, p. 43 (bottom); Alexander Wong/Getty Images, p. 43 (top).

Cover: James Hager/robertharding/Getty Images; Westend61/Getty Images; Byba Sepit/Moment/Getty Images; MSMondadori/Shutterstock.com.